MAKING THE WORLD A BETTER PLACE

by Marc O'Brian

PEARSON

Scott Foresman

Editorial Offices: Glenview, Illinois • Parsippany, New Jersey • New York, New York
Sales Offices: Needham, Massachusetts • Duluth, Georgia • Glenview, Illinois
Coppell, Texas • Ontario, California • Mesa, Arizona

ISBN: 0-328-13219-5

7 8 9 10 V010 14 13 12 11 10 09 08

The word **citizen** means to be a member of a place. The place can be a **community**, a town, a country, or it can even be the world.

So, what does it mean to be a good citizen? For one thing, it means helping others. It means trying to make the world a better place.

Children are citizens too. In what ways can children be good citizens?

These hands are the helping hands of good citizens.

Just how early can a child start being a good citizen? Well, how about at three years old?

Are you ever around three-year-olds? If you are, then you have probably heard this:

"That's mine!" and "Mommy, he's not sharing!"

No one wants to play with someone who doesn't share.

Three-year-olds have a hard time sharing and taking turns. They often want their own way. With the help of adults and older children like you, they can learn to be less **selfish**.

Not sharing makes other people feel **miserable**. Learning to share is an important step toward being a good citizen.

There are many ways that children can share and be good citizens. Some join special clubs, such as Kids Care, 4-H, or Scouts. Children in these clubs do all kinds of useful things.

Some plant trees.

Some pick up trash at the beach.

They help clean up beaches and parks. They help plant flowers and trees. They help to take care of animals in shelters. They do many other good things as well.

Some help pick up litter.

Joining a club or group is not the only way to be a good citizen. You can also be very helpful on your own. Take a look at the pictures on this page. What are the children here doing to be good citizens? How are they making the world a better place?

Do you ever do any of these things?

As children grow older, there are things they can do that really interest them and help others at the same time. For example, older children who like fish and other sea creatures can help at an **aquarium**. Those who like animals can help at the zoo. They can help care for the animals and explain things to the visitors.

Another popular way to be a good citizen is to **tutor** a younger child. To tutor means to teach. Older children can help younger children with math, reading, and doing projects.

When students turn sixteen, there are even more ways to help out. These **teenagers** can go shopping for older people. They can visit people in hospitals, serve food to hungry people, and help build houses. They can even teach sports to younger children.

When a teenager turns eighteen, there is something very special that they can do to be a good citizen. At age eighteen, people can vote. That means they have the **freedom** to choose leaders and help decide what laws there should be. Voting is an important part of being a good citizen.

At eighteen, all citizens have the right to vote.

As you have read, there are many ways to be a good citizen. Here are few more ideas.

You can help rake a sick neighbor's yard. You can work with others to help clean up your neighborhood. You can give toys to children who don't have many toys.

No matter how old you are, there are many things you can do to be a good citizen and help others.

These children collected a lot of toys to give to other children.

Now Try This

Here is a project that you can do with your classmates. You can work together to be good citizens at your school.

What can you do to make your school a better place? Talk with your classmates and come up with some ideas. Can you help clean up the school? Can you help with a project for younger children? How about putting artwork up in the halls?

Your teacher can write a list of all your ideas on the chalkboard.

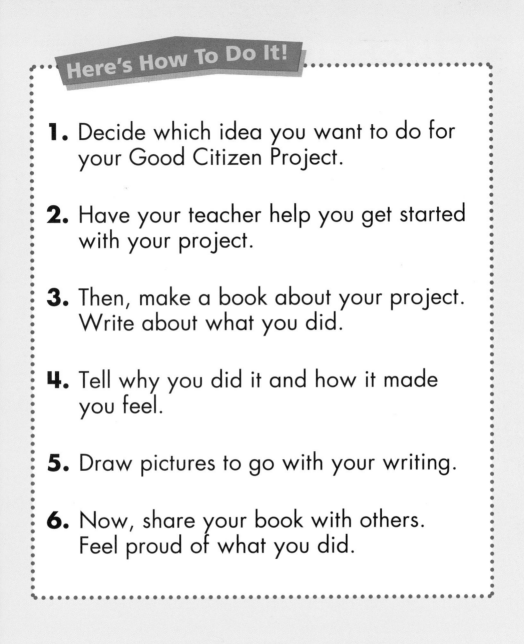

Here's How To Do It!

1. Decide which idea you want to do for your Good Citizen Project.

2. Have your teacher help you get started with your project.

3. Then, make a book about your project. Write about what you did.

4. Tell why you did it and how it made you feel.

5. Draw pictures to go with your writing.

6. Now, share your book with others. Feel proud of what you did.

Glossary

aquarium *n.* a place to keep fish and other sea life

citizen *n.* a member of a place

community *n.* a group of people who live in the same area

freedom *n.* the right to say and do what you want

miserable *adj.* sad or unhappy

selfish *adj.* to put one's own needs and wants first

teenagers *n.* people who are between thirteen and nineteen years old

tutor *v.* to teach one child at a time